LOSS OF A SPOUSE

Participant Guide

For more information:
Church Initiative
PO Box 1739
Wake Forest, NC 27588-1739
Phone: 800-395-5755 (US and Canada); 919-562-2112 (local and international)
Fax: 919-562-2114
Email: info@churchinitiative.org
Web address: www.churchinitiative.org, www.griefshare.org

WELCOME

You have begun a journey we know you did not want. We are sorry for your loss, and we want to come alongside you on this journey of grief. Our desire is to help you process your grief and think about what life after the loss of your spouse might look like.

Your life will never be the same, but we believe today's Loss of a Spouse seminar will enable you to face the future with a measure of hope.

Some of the ideas presented in Loss of a Spouse are based on Christian principles. But even if you practice a different faith, don't believe in God, or feel distant from Him, today's seminar and this participant guide can still help you. They are filled with practical information that will encourage you as you grieve, regardless of your perspective on religion.

Thank you for joining us!

In His love,

Steve Grissom
GriefShare founder and president
www.griefshare.org

CONTENTS

WHAT TO EXPECT TODAY

You might feel nervous about being here today and not sure what to expect. These feelings are normal. By the time this seminar ends, we believe you'll be glad you came!

Loss of a Spouse has three parts. Each part will help you find hope and comfort as you try to face life without your spouse.

Video

Today, you'll watch a video and hear advice from counselors and pastors (most of whom have lost a spouse). You'll also hear the stories of men and women who've been widowed and have found help and encouragement. They share honestly about topics such as:

- What to expect in the days after the loss
- The surprising emotional, physical, and spiritual effects of grief
- Challenges that surviving spouses face (e.g., loneliness, new household responsibilities, and relating to others)
- Why it won't always hurt this much
- Possibilities for hope in life

Use the note-taking section on page 1 in this guide to write comments and questions while watching the video.

Discussion

After the video, you'll have the chance to talk with others who have lost their spouses. You can discuss what you learned in the video and ask questions about any concerns you have. Please understand you do not have to share during the discussion. Because even if you don't say a word, you can still benefit from listening to others.

Participant guide

In addition to a video note-taking section, this guide contains helpful and encouraging exercises for you to read, work through, and apply to your personal situation. To get the most out of your participant guide, see "How to use this book" (p. viii).

HOW TO USE THIS BOOK

At this time in your life, it probably seems like chaos and uncertainty rule the day. The passing of your spouse affects every area of your life. Household responsibilities increase; loneliness strikes more frequently; future dreams have to be changed; and everyday stresses seem even more annoying or overwhelming.

This guide will help you understand your grief and find comfort and direction during this time of pain and uncertainty.

Be patient with your progress

We cannot say how much time it will take before the pain and uncertainty in your life subside. But they will. So be patient with yourself and with the changes that will come in your life.

Use this guide to move forward, one day at a time. And yet, as much as this guide will help you, it will take you only so far on your journey of grief. Attending a GriefShare group regularly will give you opportunities to process your loss with other grieving people. Visit **www.griefshare.org** to find a group near you.

There is no time frame in which the exercises in this book need to be completed. Grief has a way of magnifying the burdens in your life, so taking your time working with these exercises is wise. You might first read through a page a day. Decide whether the exercise on that page is relevant for your experience with grief. Then try it out. Or, you might find that you want to work on an exercise more than one day. It's up to you. The speed at which you work through the exercises is not as important as taking steps to understand and work through the challenges you are facing.

WHAT IF I'M NOT SURE ABOUT GOD?

You might not be sure what you think of God right now. You might even be angry with God, wondering why He did not stop whatever your spouse went through that ended in his or her death. We agree that those questions are reasonable to ask. It's always helpful to be honest about such struggles.

Some of your questions are probably addressed in this guide, because some of the people in the Bible also had the same questions, concerns, and complaints. So, when we refer to passages in the Bible, we ask only that you consider what you might learn from other people who have wrestled with God.

WHAT IF I'M THINKING ABOUT SUICIDE?

For some grieving spouses, thoughts about their own death pass through their minds quickly. But for others, the thoughts linger.

One type of thinking focuses on a lack of zest for life, a lack of direction in life, or the loss of goals for life. There is no strong intent to take your own life, but there's not a strong motivation to do much else either. Examples might include:

- "It felt like I was empty, and I might as well die, too."
- "God, it's okay with me if You just take me, too."

If the thoughts linger, then you should set up an appointment to talk to someone about them (a pastor, counselor, physician, etc.).

Another type of thinking focuses on how you could take your own life. For example:

- Thinking about a location where you'd kill yourself
- Thinking about the method you'd use to kill yourself
- Thinking about what you'd put in a goodbye letter to relatives

If you have these thoughts, then you need to talk to someone now. Don't wait. You could go to your local hospital's emergency room. Or if you can't get there, call the National Suicide Prevention Lifeline: 1-800-273-TALK (8255). This service provides free and confidential emotional support to people in suicidal crisis or emotional distress 24 hours a day, 7 days a week, across the United States.

If you are hard of hearing, you can contact the Lifeline via TTY by dialing 800-799-4889.

There is always someone to talk to. You don't need to face your pain by yourself.

ABOUT GRIEFSHARE

After a spouse's death, people around you often don't understand what you're going through. They might not know what to say and sometimes avoid you. They wish you would "cheer up." And you struggle with loneliness. That's why we created GriefShare.

GriefShare is a thirteen-week support group program for people grieving a loved one's death. The group leaders have been through grief themselves and want to share the help and hope they've found.

At GriefShare, the people there truly "get it." They know the emotions, the exhaustion, the struggle just to function at times. They don't rush or judge another person in grief, because they understand that each person's grief is unique.

At a weekly meeting you'll watch a video on a grief-related topic and hear insights from counselors, pastors, and people who've lost a loved one. Some of the topics covered are:

- How to handle overwhelming emotions
- Where to find the strength to go on
- What to expect in the days to come
- How to grieve in a way that's healthy and suited to you
- Biblical principles that help you deal with your grief

After the video is a small-group discussion time (where you are not required to talk, if you'd rather just listen). You'll also receive a take-home workbook that you can read throughout the week and find daily encouragement and practical helps.

Interested in trying out GriefShare?

To find a group near you, talk to the church that's hosting Loss of a Spouse. You can also visit **www.griefshare.org** or call **800-395-5755**.

MEET THE HOSTS

Rev. Michel Faulkner and Pam Lundell are cohosts of the Loss of a Spouse video. Both have experienced their spouse's death.

Rev. Michel Faulkner

Rev. Faulkner pastors New Horizon Church in Harlem, serving the economically and socially disadvantaged. In 2014, he lost Virginia, his wife of more than thirty years with whom he raised three children. Michel has dedicated his career, from professional football to education, to serving his community. Michel has a passion for leadership development. In his book *Restoring the American Dream*, he explains his vision and goals for future US generations.

Pam Lundell

Pam Lundell hosts the morning show for Christian broadcaster 98.5 KTIS in Minneapolis–Saint Paul, Minnesota. Her husband, John, died suddenly in 2005, leaving her a single mom. Pam says God took care of her in amazing ways as a young widow. Today, she serves on the board for the nonprofit Widow Might. Blessed to find love again with her second husband, Tim, she calls their children and grandchildren "my BFBF": "my big, fat blended family."

MEET THE EXPERTS

These counselors, pastors, and psychologists are featured in the Loss of a Spouse video. They share their wisdom from years of experience in counseling grieving people and through personal experience with grief.

Sabrina D. Black

Sabrina D. Black is CEO and clinical director of Abundant Life Counseling Center. A licensed counselor and certified addiction and biblical counselor, she helps others apply spiritual values to overcome life's challenges, including grief. www.abundantlifecounseling.webs.com

Dr. Fredrica Brooks-Davis

Dr. Brooks-Davis is the founder and executive director of Reid Temple Restoration Center, a church-based counseling center. Her husband, Teddy Davis, was diagnosed with brain cancer three months after they married. Before his death, they cofounded the Brooks-Davis Institute for Brain Cancer Awareness, where she serves as board president.

Dr. Robert DeVries

Dr. DeVries is professor emeritus of church education at Calvin Theological Seminary. His first wife of twenty-eight years died of cancer. Now remarried, he and wife Dr. Susan Zonnebelt-Smeenge work together to help people in grief and are the coauthors of many books, including *The Empty Chair: Handling Grief on Holidays and Special Occasions* and *From We to Me.*

Dr. Crawford Loritts

Dr. Loritts is senior pastor at Fellowship Bible Church in Roswell, Georgia. He has preached throughout the world and written eight books. With his wife, Karen, he is a featured speaker at family life and marriage conferences.

Dr. Deepak Reju

Dr. Reju leads biblical counseling and family ministries. He is associate pastor at Capitol Hill Baptist Church in Washington, DC. He serves as president of the board of directors for the Biblical Counseling Coalition and has published several books and articles.

H. Norman Wright

Wright is a grief therapist and certified trauma specialist. He is the author of more than seventy books, including *Experiencing Grief* and *Recovering from Losses in Life*. He experienced the deaths of his wife, son, and daughter. www.hnormanwright.com

Dr. Susan Zonnebelt-Smeenge

Dr. Zonnebelt-Smeenge is a licensed clinical psychologist. Her first husband died eighteen years after he was diagnosed with a malignant brain tumor. Now remarried, she and husband Dr. Robert DeVries work together to help people in grief and are the coauthors of many books, including *Getting to the Other Side of Grief* and *Traveling Through Grief*.

VIDEO NOTE-TAKING OUTLINE

Below is an outline of the video seminar you'll watch today.
Follow along as you view the video.

The Effects of Grief

Effects on your emotions and body

heart raceing

Effects on your memory and concentration

losing things

focus

The Unpredictability of Grief

Getting "ambushed" by grief

_____

_____

_____

_____

_____

The Challenges of Grief

Adjusting to "secondary losses"

_____

_____

_____

_____

Asking for help from others

_____

_____

_____

_____

Dealing with your spouse's possessions

_____

_____

_____

_____

Preserving friendships

_____

_____

_____

_____

Dealing with loneliness

_____

_____

_____

_____

Asking God for help

_____

_____

_____

_____

_____

Rethinking your identity and life goals

_____

_____

_____

_____

_____

A Path Forward with Grief

Relying on God's strength

_____

_____

_____

_____

_____

Facing fears

_____

_____

_____

_____

_____

Discovering GriefShare

How GriefShare can help you

_____

_____

_____

_____

_____

When others don't understand,
GRIEFSHARE IS THERE TO ENCOURAGE YOU

After the funeral, when the cards and letters have stopped coming, most people around you return to their normal lives. But your grief continues and you feel alone.

At a weekly GriefShare support group, you'll find people who understand and who want to help as you rebuild your life.

Learn more at www.griefshare.org.

GOING THROUGH GRIEF

G rief is always disorienting. Even if you anticipated your spouse's death, the reality of your loss can be surprisingly unsettling. In this section, you'll find answers to common questions about the wide range of reactions grieving spouses face.

You will learn:

- How each person's grief experience is unique
- Common physical effects of grief
- Which grief responses to avoid
- The value of occasional "grief breaks"

HOW DID MY SPOUSE
MAKE AN "IMPRINT" ON ME?

"A man leaves his father and mother and is united to his wife, and they become one flesh." (Genesis 2:24b)

The influence of intimacy

Part of human nature is the tendency to be influenced by those with whom we have a close relationship. The closer the relationship, the greater the likelihood of influence, because close relationships involve trust and appreciation of the other person.

Consider the many ways your spouse might have influenced you:

- Mannerisms (for example, verbal expressions, gestures)
- Handling of emotions
- Perspective on parenting
- Being organized (or disorganized!)
- Becoming more (or less) sociable
- Preferences in entertainment (music, TV, movies)
- Being more (or less) prompt to events
- Religious convictions
- Political views
- Handling finances (budgeting, investing, saving, donating)
- _____ *[Fill in other types of influence]*
- _____
- _____

This might help you

Do you wonder why your grief is taking so long to pass? Or, why it's so intense? If you do, consider the extent of your spouse's influence on you. You've lost a unique relationship. So don't try to rush your grief. Expect it to hurt profoundly for a season.

For now, take time to review old birthday and holiday cards, scrapbooks, photo albums, love letters, etc. These items can provide reminders of the numerous blessings your spouse brought into your life.

SHOULD I BE SURPRISED BY MY GRIEF REACTIONS?

"How long must I wrestle with my thoughts and day after day have sorrow in my heart?" (Psalm 13:2a)

The diversity of grief reactions

You might be alarmed by how your grief is affecting you. The writer of Psalm 13 was troubled by how long his sorrow lasted. Take a look at what was surprising to these grieving spouses (perhaps you can relate!):

Malika: "I was surprised by the physical pain."

Rob: "The extreme anxiety, the fear, and the uneasiness about doing the normal activities of the day took me totally by surprise."

Barbara: "I was tired constantly. I didn't care if I made dinner, or ate, or whatever."

Malika: "It was difficult to concentrate. Someone would tell me something, and I would forget it. I would have a to-do list of ten things and only get one thing done."

Grief can affect your emotions, your reasoning ability, your motivation, and your body. And you won't necessarily experience grief in the same way each time you lose someone close to you. The varied and often surprising effects of grief are disorienting and troubling, but, fortunately, they are also temporary.

This might help you

Since everyone's reaction to grief is different, you may be struggling with different questions than others who are using this guide. So don't feel the need to read this book in order. Look through the contents page and select the sections that would be most helpful to you.

To determine if your reactions to your spouse's death are typical, see "Is my grief normal?" (p. 57).

WHAT'S GOING ON
WITH MY BODY?

"Be merciful to me, LORD, for I am in distress; my eyes grow weak
with sorrow, my soul and body with grief." (Psalm 31:9)

The unexpected physical effects of grief

In the Loss of a Spouse video you met Ronett, Barbara, and Malika.
Ronett was worried about her physical weaknesses after her husband's
death. And the stress of grief worsened her skin problems and asthma.
You, too, can be prone to increased physical problems, because grief
greatly stresses your body.

You might find it difficult to sleep, producing fatigue and difficulties with
memory and concentration. Barbara said: "I was so tired. I didn't have the
energy to do anything." Or maybe you're sleeping much more than normal.
And then, when you're awake, you have no desire to leave the bed.

In addition, some grieving people have headaches and sore muscles
resulting from the tension associated with grief. Malika was surprised by
stomach and chest pains.

This might help you

As you grieve, don't neglect taking care of your body:

- Try to get proper nutrition. Be sure to drink adequate amounts
  of water.[1]

- Try to get enough sleep (7–8 hours per night). In addition, lie down
  2–3 times a day for 20–30 minutes, even if you don't sleep.

- Try to take a 10-to-20-minute walk each day, depending on your
  level of fitness. If you are able, try other types of exercise: biking,
  swimming, playing tennis, etc. With a variety of exercises, you are
  more likely to stick with it.

- Set up reminders so you don't forget to take any prescription
  medications.

- If you have new pains or other symptoms, make an appointment
  with your physician.

1 For some guidelines on how much water you should drink each day, search the Mayo
   Clinic's website: www.mayoclinic.org.

WHY DOES MY GRIEF COME OUT OF NOWHERE?

"Save me, O God, for the waters have come up to my neck." (Psalm 69:1)

If you were to stand in the ocean, every so often a wave would swell and hit you. Some of the waves would be tall and powerful, strong enough to knock you off balance. Other waves would be smaller, and their impact would not be as noticeable. And if you faced the shore, you wouldn't know when the waves would hit you.

Grief will ebb and flow for a while

In some ways, grief works like the waves in the ocean. Holidays, birthdays, and anniversaries are common times for grief waves to crash against you. You may recall that Rob was knocked off balance by such a "grief wave" on his wife's birthday. Waves of grief can also hit you at unexpected times. Eleanor said she can get teary-eyed even ten years after her husband's death at restaurants they'd enjoyed going to together.

This might help you

Grief waves are especially common in the first year. Here are some suggestions for surviving those difficult days (anniversaries, birthdays, holidays):

- Take off work if you can.
- Do something that you can enjoy by yourself. Pick an activity that might become a new tradition for you.
- Spend the time reminiscing with people who shared a love for your spouse. Don't hesitate to take initiative with your friends. They will appreciate the opportunity to comfort you.
- Don't overextend yourself. For example, for holiday gatherings, limit how much hosting, baking, or shopping you do. Allow yourself some downtime afterward.
- Participate in a GriefShare group. The people you meet and the insights you gain can be a tremendous source of encouragement for anniversaries, birthdays, and holidays. You can find a group at **www.griefshare.org**.

WHAT IF I CAN'T STOP CRYING?

"This is why I weep and my eyes overflow with tears."
(Lamentations 1:16a)

Understand why you cry

Crying is a natural grief response observed in people around the world. How much you cry is affected by a number of factors:

- Temperament: You might be someone who is simply "wired" to express emotions more easily.

- Social setting: How close you are to others in the setting will affect how likely you are to cry.

- Comfort level for crying in public: What you were taught growing up about the "public display of emotions" will affect how much you cry.

- Experiences in life: Your experiences in life can change how easily you cry now.

There are several potential benefits to crying. Crying might act like a stress reliever for your body. It certainly alerts others to your struggle so they are more likely to offer you assistance. So, if you feel like crying, it's okay.

This might help you

If you feel uncomfortable crying in public, then you might consider finding a secluded spot to cry. Some people like to set aside a certain time of the day to cry; then if tears well up at other times of the day, they remind themselves about their scheduled crying time and try to distract themselves in the meantime.

IS IT OKAY
IF I DON'T CRY?

Crying is a common grief response. So, you might wonder if there is a problem if you are not crying much in your grief.

Some people don't cry as much as others

There is no need to be concerned if you are not prone to cry. A lack of tears does not necessarily mean you are less sad than other people who grieve. A number of factors affect how much you cry:

- Temperament: You might not be "wired" to cry that easily.

- Social setting: You might not be that close to other people around you, which will make it harder to cry.

- Comfort level for crying in public: You might have been taught that it's not appropriate to have strong displays of emotion in public.

Not everyone who cries actually feels better afterward. Crying can be a stress reliever for the body, but not everyone processes stress the same way.

This might help you

If you don't feel the urge to cry, that's okay. What's more important than producing tears is coming to terms with the significance of your loss. The exercises in this book will help you do that.

CAN I NUMB MY PAIN?

"But as for me, my feet had almost slipped;
I had nearly lost my foothold." (Psalm 73:2)

Unhelpful responses to grief

Your grief can be very intense. So, it's natural for you to want relief from the discomfort. However, avoid those behaviors that only distract you from the pain temporarily. For example:

- Shopping binges
- Sex
- Alcohol/drugs
- Overeating
- Workaholism
- Sitting in front of the TV for hours alone

None of these activities will help you in the long run. In fact, they are likely to create more complications for you.

This might help you

1. For *two weeks*: Every time you are tempted toward your unhelpful responses to grief, answer the following questions.

   - What thoughts and feelings are troubling you? Be as specific as possible.
   - What advantages and disadvantages can come if you continue this behavior?
   - What other, more productive, behavior could you use to replace the unhelpful behavior?

2. Use these reflections to talk to your pastor, physician, or other appropriate professional about your specific struggle.

HOW HARD SHOULD I WORK AT DEALING WITH MY GRIEF?

"There is a time for everything, and a season for every activity under the heavens ... a time to weep and a time to laugh, a time to mourn and a time to dance." (Ecclesiastes 3:1, 4)

Refueling for your grief journey

Grief-focused journaling, reminiscing with photographs, and distributing your spouse's possessions are all important "mile markers" on your journey of grief. But they are also very taxing, aren't they?

That's why it's wise to take periodic breaks from grief-related activities. These breaks are simply brief diversions that will help "refuel" you for going further on your journey, like you would stop occasionally for gas and a meal on a road trip.

This might help you

Here are some guidelines for your brief grief breaks:

- Plan something you enjoy each day. You might set aside time to read a good book, watch a favorite sitcom, eat a sweet treat you don't normally eat, etc. Rob, in the video, found that building scale models was a relaxing distraction from his intense struggles with grief. Like Rob, think of activities that easily capture your attention. Since these are times for personal nurture, don't plan group activities for this purpose.

- Plan "mini-vacations" that do not take a lot of time or money, but that help you reconnect with life. You might choose activities that you can enjoy by yourself or with others. For example, you could get a massage, go for a Sunday drive to explore an unfamiliar area, spend a night at a bed and breakfast, go to a museum or a sporting event, take a bike ride with a friend, etc. Ronett took a martial arts class every Monday evening. Malika schedules "pampering days" every couple of weeks and gets her hair and nails done.

AM I STAYING BUSY TO AVOID MY GRIEF?

"Be still, and know that I am God." (Psalm 46:10a)

The allure of busyness

Some people find it incredibly difficult to get motivated to do anything after their spouse dies. But others find they can't sit still; if you are this way, be aware of the trap of using busyness to avoid thinking about how your life must change. This kind of busyness is a trap because you can accomplish tasks, which feels good. But when you don't have anything left to do, the emptiness feels suffocating.

Recognizing the busyness trap

It's also important to recognize that this busyness is not the same as the brief grief breaks we described on page 16. Grief breaks are short periods of time in which you intentionally focus on activities or people that don't remind you of your loss. Busyness is a desperate effort to avoid dealing with the reality of your loss.

This might help you

Be sure you're not caught in the busyness trap. If you're not certain, ask trusted, honest friends to tell you if you are. If you recall, Barbara's daughter helped Barbara realize she was getting "stuck" in her grief because of busyness.

Common concerns of grieving spouses:

DEALING WITH LONELINESS AND ANXIETY

Your life was shaped by your spouse's company, advice, and protection. There was a sense of security that you no longer have. In this section, you'll hear answers to questions about living alone.

You will learn:

- How being lonely and being alone are not the same thing
- The important difference between isolation and solitude
- Other people's roles in helping to decrease your anxiety (and where God fits in)

HOW CAN I DEAL
WITH MY LONELINESS?

"Turn to me and be gracious to me, for I am lonely."
(Psalm 25:16a)

Being lonely vs. being alone

Addressing loneliness is a difficult and ongoing challenge after the loss of your spouse.

You can feel lonely even when others are present with you. For example, have you ever been invited to a party and then when you got there, you realized everyone else was part of a couple? If you don't feel a connection with others in the room, then loneliness is the result.

It's also true that you can be completely alone in a room and yet *not* feel lonely. At these times, you are comfortable being with just yourself. Generally speaking, these also are times when you are doing something you enjoy or find profitable.

This might help you

To deal with loneliness, then, you will need to build relationships with others and do things that you enjoy. Here are some suggestions to get you started:

- Engage in activities that you've enjoyed in the past, which involve other people. In the video, Eleanor looked for community volunteer opportunities, and Fred joined a gym. Or maybe there's a new activity you've always wanted to learn.

- Look for a GriefShare group near you. You can look for one on the website **www.griefshare.org**. You'll meet people who can relate to your struggles and offer emotional support.

- Prepare for those times when your loneliness might be especially difficult. Malika purposefully plans outings for her weekends and then invites friends to join her.

- Resume your hobbies (or start new ones). You won't always be able to surround yourself with friends and family. Find things you enjoy doing alone to keep you from focusing on the fact that you aren't with others.

WHY DO I NEED TO SPEND TIME WITH OTHERS?

"Two are better than one, because they have good return for their labor: If either of them falls down, one can help the other up.... Also, if two lie down together, they will keep warm. But how can one keep warm alone?... A cord of three strands is not quickly broken." (Ecclesiastes 4:9–12)

The benefits of community

You probably can relate to the sentiment in the passage above. As you think about your spouse, you are reminded that "two are better than one." But does the same idea also apply to recovering from your grief? Would you benefit from a grief support group?

Maybe you're thinking you'd rather be alone than risk an emotional outburst in front of others or have to answer unwanted or insensitive questions. But, in fact, there are many good reasons for finding a supportive community of grievers as part of dealing with your grief:

- You will hear ideas from other grieving spouses about how to deal with practical issues you might be facing.
- You can develop friendships with people.
- You can have someone to keep you accountable so that you are less likely to make unwise choices.
- You get the chance to hear how others, further along on their grief journeys, have been able to look ahead in their lives (to see life from a different perspective).

This might help you

Look for a GriefShare group near you. You can use the Find a Group search tool at **www.griefshare.org**.

WHAT SHOULD I DO WITH MY ALONE TIME?

"I have become like a bird alone on a roof." (Psalm 102:7b)

Isolation vs. solitude

In the Loss of a Spouse video, Eleanor made a helpful distinction between isolation and solitude. "Solitude is when you need some time just to be alone with your memories, with your thoughts, and with the Lord. But isolation is totally different. That's when you begin to shut people out of your life."

Choosing to be alone can be helpful, as long as you aren't simply avoiding how your loss affects your life. Choosing to be alone so that you have time to reflect on the blessings from your marriage or on making changes in your life is valuable.

This might help you

Plan regular times in your schedule for some reflective solitude. Here are some suggestions for your plan:

- Take some time specifically for reflective solitude. Dr. DeVries set aside blocks of a few hours twice a week, during which he would look at photos, read old letters, and listen to soothing music.

- Pick a place where you won't be interrupted. You might also consider a place of special significance. For example, since Barbara enjoys working with flowers, she spends time "playing in her garden." It's a place of refuge where she can have conversations with the Lord.

- Use this guide to structure your times of solitude. Plan regular times when you might complete activities like the ones in this guide. This will eliminate the need to figure out what to do during your times of solitude.

WHAT IF I'M ANXIOUS ABOUT MOVING INTO THE FUTURE?

"Cast all your anxiety on him because he cares for you." (1 Peter 5:7)

An uncertain future

Soon after Rob lost his wife, he was shocked by the anxiety that suddenly hounded him day after day. He struggled even with going on bike rides, going to the grocery store, and going to a barber. Anxiety is a common part of people's grief experiences because the future is unfamiliar and uncertain.

Less stability for the future

Ronett and Marisol had been stay-at-home moms. When their husbands died, they wondered how they would make it financially. They acquired all the household responsibilities that their husbands had taken care of, and they didn't know how to do many of them. Their husbands had been strong, stabilizing influences in their lives.

You, too, may be missing the help, encouragement, counsel, and assurance that your spouse gave you. You might have to figure out how to do chores you never wanted to do. And it's reasonable to wonder, "How can I possibly move forward into this unfamiliar and uncertain future?"

This might help you

Don't hesitate to ask the trustworthy people in your life for assistance with specific tasks. Encourage them to be realistic and honest as they assess their availability to help you. And make sure that your expectations of the amount (and type) of help they might give are realistic, too.

Also consider asking your helpers if they could teach you their skills as you look toward the future. As you gain more knowledge and develop more skills, there will be fewer triggers for anxiety.

Finally, tell God what worries you. First Peter 5:7 encourages us to share our anxieties with God because He cares for us. Take Him up on His offer.[2]

---

2 To learn more about having a relationship with God, see "How can I have hope?" (p. 53).

GRIEF SHARE LOSS OF A SPOUSE

WILL IT HELP
IF I GO TO GOD?

"I will say of the LORD, 'He is my refuge and my fortress,
my God, in whom I trust.'" (Psalm 91:2)

The psalm writers experienced tragedies and knew great sorrow. Even though this sometimes left them confused and overwhelmed by grief, they knew that God loved and cared for them. So even when God did not seem to make sense to them, they realized they ultimately needed to go to Him for help.

It wasn't necessarily easy for them to approach God, because they did not know how He would respond to their pleas. But they moved toward Him because of His history of aiding those in need over the centuries.

"We wait in hope for the LORD; he is our help and our shield. In him our hearts rejoice, for we trust in his holy name. May your unfailing love be with us, LORD, even as we put our hope in you."

Psalm 33:20–22

"I am counting on the LORD; yes, I am counting on him. I have put my hope in his word [his promises]."

Psalm 130:5 NLT

This might help you

God is the same now as He was then. Hebrews 11:6 says "he rewards those who earnestly seek him." Just as the psalmists reached out to Him, so can you.[3]

---

3 To read more about how much God loves you, see "How can I have hope?" (p. 53).

WHO WILL GUIDE OR PROTECT ME NOW?

"But you, LORD, are a shield around me." (Psalm 3:3a)

Sometimes your path in life takes you places you'd rather not go. Illnesses, accidents, lost jobs … the loss of a spouse. And during those times it's normal to feel vulnerable. To comfort you, Psalm 23 presents a picture of God as a caring shepherd:

"He guides me along the right paths for his name's sake.
Even though I walk through the darkest valley,[4]
I will fear no evil, for you are with me;
your rod and your staff, they comfort me."
Psalm 23:3–4

The Shepherd leads His sheep in tough times

In the author's word picture, he presents a deep ravine with high, steep, rocky cliffs on both sides. The sun's light is scarce, so there are plenty of shadows, where predators and thieves could lie waiting. Whatever trial he was facing at that time, that's the image that came to mind. Can you relate to such an anxiety-provoking image? Do you wonder what problems "lie waiting" in the future?

This might help you

The author also imagines God guiding and protecting him through the dark valley with the standard tools of a shepherd: a rod and a staff. With the staff a shepherd directed the movements of the sheep. With the rod (a short club) a shepherd could beat off attackers. That image comforted him; his fears were alleviated as he thought of the Lord watching over him. Take some time to think about how you relate to that image.

---

4 You may have heard this translated "the valley of the shadow of death."

GRIEF SHARE LOSS OF A SPOUSE

I FEEL LOST RIGHT NOW;
WHERE CAN I GO?

God invites you to stay with Him

Grief is exhausting. What's worse, you often have no idea how long your journey of grief will last. Knowing you'd feel that way, the end of Psalm 23 describes God as a host who takes in a worn-out, weary traveler.

"You prepare a table before me in the presence of my enemies. You anoint my head with oil; my cup overflows.
Surely your goodness and love will follow me all the days of my life, and I will dwell in the house of the LORD forever."

Psalm 23:5–6

God is the perfect host, taking you in during a tough, stressful time. In those days, the host was expected to feed and protect the people he received. He was also expected to offer travelers oil to refresh their chapped skin (common for travelers exposed to the sun and dry wind). God offers you the same refreshment for your soul.

There's room in the house of the Lord

The author of the psalm knew God's goodness and love would always be available to him. When God opens His "house" to worn-out, weary travelers, *no one needs to leave.* God's resources and His love are limitless.

This might help you

Maybe right now your grief makes it hard to see evidence of God's goodness and love. In the midst of the changes in your life, look for the signs of a "new normal," such as:

- Waking up on a morning when grief is not the first thing you think of
- Eating a meal that tastes good again
- Sleeping a little better than the night before
- Smiling again at others' dry wit.

Those experiences are all evidence of God's goodness and love following—*pursuing*—you.[5] As you recognize them, we encourage you to make it a habit to thank the Lord and, with the author of Psalm 23, to "dwell in the house of the LORD forever."[6]

5 James 1:17: "Every good and perfect gift is from above, coming down from the Father of the heavenly lights, who does not change like shifting shadows."
6 For more information about the extent of God's love, see "How can I have hope?" (p. 53).

CAN I REALLY BE
HONEST WITH GOD?

"My God, my God … Why are you so far from … my cries of anguish?
My God, I cry out by day, but you do not answer." (Psalm 22:1–2a)

Being real with God

In some ways, reading the book of Psalms in the Bible is like reading someone's diary. You read honest statements of struggle between the psalm writers and God, such as in Psalm 22 above. When you read different psalms, you'll get examples of how people talked to God about their pain. For example:

"My soul is in deep anguish.

How long, LORD, how long?"

Psalm 6:3

Pastor Loritts said, "The presence of struggle does not mean that your faith is weak. The presence of struggle does not mean you're not a spiritual person because you feel pain and disappointment."

This might help you

God understands that you are going through emotional turmoil. You can go to Him with the hurt (or anxiety or anger). Ask Him for the strength to persevere. If you'd like some guidance, here are some sample prayers. Just fill in the details about your particular struggles.

Lord, I hurt so much right now. I miss _____ so much.
I miss the way he/she _____. I regret that we won't be able to _____. I just feel lost right now. Lord, please help me with _____. Thanks for being there for me, Lord.

Lord, I'm angry. I don't understand why _____ died at this time, in this way. It makes no sense to me. I don't know what I'm going to do. Will You please help me? Help me to see whom I might talk to about _____. Help me not to hold a grudge. Thanks for being willing to hear me out, Lord.

WEEKLY ENCOURAGEMENT
as you rebuild your life

At weekly GriefShare support groups, you will find friendly,
caring people who will walk alongside you through
one of life's most difficult experiences.
You don't have to go through the grieving process alone.

Learn more at www.griefshare.org.

MOVING FORWARD

The loss of your spouse requires changes in your life. You might need to address some aspects of the past so you are freer to move forward. You will need to take stock of the resources you have that will enable you to move into the future, step by step. In this section, you'll get answers to your questions about taking those initial steps.

You will learn how to:

- Deal with the emotional impact of past conflicts with your spouse
- Take on your new household responsibilities
- Preserve memories of your spouse
- Look at and think about the future

WHAT DO I DO WITH "UNFINISHED BUSINESS" WITH MY SPOUSE? (PART 1)

"Who can say, 'I have kept my heart pure;
I am clean and without sin'?" (Proverbs 20:9)

No one is perfect

No marriage is perfect. And you can likely think of things you wish you'd handled differently when you had the chance: conflicts left unresolved, inappropriate words used in frustration, etc. So how do you deal with such "unfinished business" when your spouse is no longer present?

You can't resolve the unfinished business in your marriage, but you can learn and grow personally because of it. To do so, you need to be honest about how both you and your spouse contributed to the relationship problems.

This might help you

You might not be ready to think about the conflicts in your marriage or times when you or your spouse didn't handle things well. And that's okay. But when you are ready, it will be valuable for you to answer the question below. (And you might need input from another person who is trustworthy and familiar with your marriage.)

Start by identifying the issues that you wish both you and your spouse had handled better in your marriage: What two or three conflicts were really significant to you? (You'll use these responses to complete part 2 of this exercise.)

1. _____

2. _____

3. _____

WHAT DO I DO WITH "UNFINISHED BUSINESS" WITH MY SPOUSE? (PART 2)

"Be kind and compassionate to one another,
forgiving each other...." (Ephesians 4:32a)

The Bible's call to forgive

Forgiveness is a critically important element in all relationships, because we all say and do things that can hurt others. A lack of forgiveness (that is, holding a grudge) can prolong your grief. However, there's even more at stake. "But if you do not forgive others their sins, your Father will not forgive your sins" (Matthew 6:15).[7]

Forgiveness is a commitment

So what does it mean to forgive? To forgive means making a commitment not to hold other people's offenses (sins) against them. Ideally, forgiveness happens between two people in order to preserve the relationship. But what if the other person is not available, such as your spouse?

This might help you

Jesus alludes to the situation of forgiving when the other person isn't present in Mark 11:25. He says to His disciples, "When you stand praying, if you hold anything against anyone, forgive them [in your heart]." While that's as far as you can go with forgiving your spouse, the benefits are still very real.

Refer back to the list of issues that led to conflict between you and your spouse (see page 33). Then forgive your spouse for the ways that he or she contributed to each conflict. If you have difficulty forgiving because of the severity of your spouse's offenses (or any other reason), talk to a pastor or Christian counselor about your concerns.

---

7 To learn how you can experience God's forgiveness for your contribution to the conflict between you and your spouse, read "Receiving God's forgiveness" (p. 60).

WHAT HELP DO I
NEED RIGHT NOW?

Your spouse probably took care of many household and family responsibilities. These roles now fall on you. To make this more manageable, think about which responsibilities you are comfortable with and which ones you are not comfortable with at this time. This will enable you to plan ahead so that the responsibilities don't pile up for you.

This might help you

Use this checklist to take stock of what you can do now and what you will need help with.

Role	"I can do this"	"I could use some help"
Carpenter		
Checkbook balancer		
Clothes washer		
Cook/baker		
Co-parent		
Electrician		
Garden/yard worker		
House cleaner		
Interior decorator		
Mechanic		
Nurse		
Plumber		
Shopper		
Other:		
Other:		
Other:		

The next few pages offer further suggestions to help you with your immediate needs.

WHO MIGHT BE AVAILABLE TO HELP ME?

"Blessed is the one who is kind to the needy." (Proverbs 14:21b)

Because of the upheaval in your life now, it would be a good idea to enlist some help from others.

It's not what you know, but who you know

Write a list of all the people who would likely offer support if asked. Consider family, friends, neighbors, coworkers, fellow church members, and people in other organizations you're a part of.

Then label each person on the list with one or more of these letters:

- *L* – those who are good *listeners*
- *D* – those who are *doers* (individuals with the skills and/or tools needed to do various jobs you're not yet skilled to do)
- *R* – those who can offer *relaxation* from the tasks associated with grief (they are the ones you hang out with for a good laugh or a mutually enjoyed activity, but who may not be comfortable talking with you about your grief)[8]

Names	L, D, or R?

---

8 This exercise is suggested by Kenneth J. Doka, *Grief Is a Journey* (New York: Atria Books, 2016), 114.

HOW DO I ASSEMBLE A SUPPORT NETWORK?

"Whoever is kind to the needy honors God." (Proverbs 14:31b)

Taking inventory

After you determine who can help you, you should refine your list so that you know who's the best person to ask for help in any situation. Below are ten descriptions of different types of people who could offer support as you grieve.

Look at the names of the people you listed in the exercise "Who might be available to help me?" (p. 36). Place the names under every description below that applies (some names might be repeated several times, others not at all).[9]

1. Someone who is available to spend time with you.
   Names: _____
   _____

2. Someone comfortable with your tears.
   Names: _____
   _____

3. Someone willing to listen to you, *repeatedly.* The person understands that it will take time for you to process the many ways your loss will affect you over the course of weeks or months.
   Names: _____
   _____

4. Someone known to be kind, gracious, and patient with others.
   Names: _____
   _____

5. Someone who understands you might be angry about your loss, but who can gently remind you of the dangers of resentment.
   Names: _____
   _____

---

9 Once you are part of a GriefShare group, you will be in a wonderful place to find names for your list. To find a group, visit **www.griefshare.org**.

6. Someone willing to ask questions that draw out your thoughts.
    Names: _____

7. Someone who appreciates the challenge that your fears bring
    to your life, but who also can remind you of the ways you've
    overcome them in the past.
    Names: _____

8. Someone who can help you see the strengths and resources you
    have available to help you forge a new life.
    Names: _____

9. Someone who can provide occasional distractions from the new
    challenges you are facing.
    Names: _____

10. Someone who has experienced a life-altering loss (through death,
    divorce, a move, a natural disaster, etc.) and was able to reorient
    his or her life afterward.
    Names: _____

Once you have finished placing the names on your list, contact each of
the people with specific requests. For example:

- For the *listeners*, ask to meet for coffee or a meal so that you can talk
  about "life." Assure them you are not looking for a counselor, but a
  sounding board. You are looking for someone who would be willing to
  listen and to help you process what life might look like from now on.

- For the *doers*, ask if they can help you with those tasks they are
  skilled at performing. Suggest a few times for them to do the tasks
  in the beginning. Let them know that eventually you would like to
  learn how to do these tasks yourself.

- For the *relaxation-companions*, ask when they might be available for
  whatever activity you envision doing with them.

WHAT ARE MY PERSONAL STRENGTHS? (PART 1)

"For you created my inmost being; you knit me together in my mother's womb. I praise you because I am fearfully and wonderfully made." (Psalm 139:13–14a)

Looking beyond the losses

Right now you probably spend more time thinking about what you do not have in your life. And that's to be expected. But while it may not seem like it now, at some point you'll begin thinking about making adjustments. When you do, taking stock of your personal strengths will be important.

Knowing your strengths will help you decide when to ask for help and what responsibilities you can handle on your own. Personal strengths include your natural talents, positive character traits, and learned skills.

This might help you

Use these questions to help you identify your personal strengths.

1. What strengths helped me get through past hard times in my life?

_____

_____

_____

_____

_____

2. What are some things I've been able to do since my spouse died that I'd never considered doing in the past?

_____

_____

_____

_____

_____

_____

WHAT ARE MY PERSONAL STRENGTHS? (PART 2)

Just as your experience of grief is unique, so will be your path forward through your grief. You certainly can learn from other people's ways of dealing with grief, but your goal shouldn't be to copy them. This is why recognizing your personal strengths is important. Using your strengths enables you to gradually move forward.

Where to look for your strengths

Your personal strengths include:

- Your natural talents: the ranges of abilities that are part of God's design for you. These are the abilities you are particularly drawn to and that usually come easy to you. For example, are you artistic? Logical and organized? Sensitive to the needs of others?

- Your learned skills: the abilities you've taken the time to learn, usually because of a need in your life. For example, reading, driving a car, cooking, using power tools, etc.

- Your positive character traits: the values that shape how you use your talents and skills to accomplish goals that you consider worthwhile. For example, kindness, honesty, humility, self-control, gentleness, etc.

Ways personal strengths can be helpful

Recognizing these personal strengths reminds you that you have something to work with as you make adjustments in your life. For example:

- Susan, who loves to learn, read as much as she could about grief to feel prepared for what she might experience.

- Norm, who has a flair for writing, began journaling about his grief, which helped him deal with the sense of chaos grief created in his life.

- Fred, who had always been an organizer/planner, found a strategy that guided how he made changes in his life.

- Barbara, who had always enjoyed serving others, looked for ways to reconnect with people who needed help in their lives.

This might help you

Here are some more questions that can help you identify your strengths:

1. What are some *past* accomplishments of mine? (Think about goals you've achieved at work, skills you've learned, successes with hobbies, and contributions you've made in your community or in your family and friends' lives.)

    _____

    _____

    _____

    _____

    _____

    _____

2. What strengths did I use to accomplish those things?

    _____

    _____

    _____

    _____

    _____

3. What strengths have others noticed in my life? (If you aren't sure, then ask people who know you well.)

    _____

    _____

    _____

    _____

    _____

    _____

WHAT ABOUT TASKS THAT REMIND ME OF MY SPOUSE?

"Have I not commanded you? Be strong and courageous." (Joshua 1:9a)

Avoidance can be costly

You might find yourself avoiding activities that you associate with your spouse. Some of these activities might not be necessary in your life, and choosing to avoid them is fine. However, others cannot be avoided for very long without creating problems for you, such as dealing with financial matters, taking care of home or car repairs, and preparing meals for yourself.

This might help you

1. Maybe you've been able to avoid some tasks that remind you of your spouse. But it's important to assess the consequences of avoiding them. Answer these questions:

- Which activities have you been avoiding specifically because they remind you of your spouse?

_____

_____

_____

_____

- How has avoiding these activities made things hard for you?

_____

_____

_____

_____

2. If you need to complete tasks that you've been avoiding, you might be able to pace yourself as you do it. Other people might initially be available to do the activities for you. But create a plan to incorporate those activities into your routine. Begin with small steps, but *take the steps*. If necessary, ask another person to help you.

WHAT DO I DO WITH ALL MY SPOUSE'S BELONGINGS?

"If any of you lacks wisdom, you should ask God, who gives generously to all without finding fault, and it will be given to you." (James 1:5)

A difficult task

Dealing with your spouse's personal belongings is a very difficult task. It does not need to be done right away or all at once. You might enlist others to help you, but it is important that *you* make the final decisions. That will lower the risk of not keeping something that is important to you.

This might help you

Fred used the following strategy for dealing with his wife's belongings, which you might adapt for your situation:

- Put some of your spouse's belongings in containers, like plastic tubs or cardboard boxes. Place the containers where you will see them regularly. Fred chose the entryway of his house.

- Also place a few empty containers in the hallway. Label one with your name. Label other containers with the names of family members or friends of your spouse who might appreciate a memento. Have another container labeled "I Don't Know."

- When you are ready, redistribute the mementos in the appropriately labeled containers. Contact the people who will get the mementos.

- You might keep the "I Don't Know" container longer. Eventually, you can decide if you want to keep or give away the items in it.

WILL IT HELP IF I HELP OTHERS?

"Let each of you look not only to his own interests,
but also to the interests of others." (Philippians 2:4 ESV)

The blessing of giving to others

Remember in the video how Barbara rediscovered a purpose for her life by serving others through the flower shop and GriefShare? Fred mentored prisoners. And Ronett found new strength as she reached out to children in her church.

By God's grand design, when people serve others in love, it also benefits the one doing the serving. In fact, Jesus said, "It is more blessed [personally rewarding] to give than to receive" (Acts 20:35).

One of the most familiar phrases in the Bible comes from Matthew 7:12. Jesus says, "So in everything, do to others what you would have them do to you." Jesus' message is simple: rather than thinking only about what other people can do for you, reach out to help others.

This might help you

As you progress on your journey of grief, you should consider this same counsel. Earlier in the guide you took stock of your personal strengths and your social network. So you know *how* you can serve and *whom* you can serve. Now all you need is a plan to "do unto others." Take time to match your resources and abilities to the needs of others you know. Then, reach out and be blessed!

1. I could serve _____

by _____ .

2. I could serve _____

by _____ .

3. I could serve _____

by _____ .

GRIEFSHARE LOSS OF A SPOUSE

HOW CAN I PRESERVE
THE MEMORIES OF MY SPOUSE?

"For this reason a man will leave his father and mother and be united to his wife, and the two will become one flesh." (Ephesians 5:31)

The value of preserving memories

Although you can no longer enjoy your spouse's company, your life can still be enriched because of the relationship you had together.

Norm Wright strongly urges grieving spouses to take steps to preserve the memories of their marriages. Typically, preserving memories involves more than merely talking about the past with others. Our memories are not like video recorders: they do not maintain footage of the past with certainty. They can fade and even change over time.

This might help you

That's why it's helpful to preserve memories in some physical form. Here are some possibilities. (Don't be discouraged if you can't do these activities right away.)

- Create a scrapbook of photos organized by themes (for example, hobbies, achievements, vacations), including some written notes for the photos.
- Use your spouse's mementos (for example, trophies, awards, or artwork) to create a display for your house.
- Digitize old videos for longer-term viewing.
- Use articles of clothing to make (or ask someone to make) a quilt, pillow, or stuffed animal.
- Record what other people remember about your spouse's contributions to their lives.

Completing one or more of these activities (or perhaps a different activity that suits your interests and skills) will help you hold on to the precious memories of your spouse.

WHAT TYPE OF THINKING WILL HELP ME MOVE FORWARD IN MY LIFE?

"Be transformed by the renewing of your mind." (Romans 12:2a)

Resilience in grief

Researchers tell us that resilient people—those who regularly recover from upsets in their lives—think about life in a certain way.[10] For example, resilient people are open to seeing new possibilities when their old routines are disrupted. They are able to see—and be thankful for—small pleasures in their lives.

These ways of thinking make it easier to deal with challenges in life. So it shouldn't surprise us to learn that God encourages us to monitor our thinking. Let's just say that He knew about the importance of our thought life long before researchers discovered it.

Useful thinking

This is why the Bible says, "Whatever is true, whatever is noble, whatever is right, whatever is pure, whatever is lovely, whatever is admirable—if anything is excellent or praiseworthy—think about such things" (Philippians 4:8). In a sense, this verse sets boundaries for your thoughts so they don't stray into unhelpful territory.

If your thoughts do stray outside these boundaries, that will hinder you as you try to move forward. But before we take a closer look at how this verse might help you, let's first consider what Paul, the author of Philippians 4:8, means by each term or "boundary."

The Boundaries: "Whatever Is …"	Your Thinking Should Be …
True	Focused on what is verified or honest, rather than on what is speculated or false
Noble	Focused on what is worthwhile and respectable, rather than what is trivial or pointless Continued …

10 For example, Lucy Hone, *Resilient Grieving* (New York: The Experiment, 2017).

The Boundaries: "Whatever Is ..."	Your Thinking Should Be ...
Right (in the sense of "just")	Focused on what is required in a situation or due to others, rather than avoiding duties
Pure	Focused on what is not tainted by evil (selfish) motives
Lovely	Focused on what is well thought of by others
Admirable	Focused on what is likely to win over others, rather than offend them
Excellent/praiseworthy	Focused on what God would approve of

This might help you

Write Philippians 4:8 or the chart on an index card that you can keep with you. When you are tempted to dwell on pessimistic, irritating, or anxious thoughts, use it to redirect your thinking.

For example, let's say you're wrestling with the thought, "I will be alone for the rest of my life." While it is true that your spouse is gone, this statement rigidly assumes there won't be any other new close relationships in the future. No one can replace your spouse, but other relationships—those with friends (new or old) and family—can ease some of the burden of your spouse not being present.

Think about friends and family members who have supported you in your grief. Those relationships have the potential to change and grow deeper in the coming years.

In addition, remind yourself of God's promises to His children,[11] such as: "I will never fail you. I will never abandon you" (Hebrews 13:5 NLT). Nothing can separate us from "the love of God that is in Christ Jesus" (Romans 8:39).

---

11 God's children are those who are part of His family by receiving the forgiveness offered through Jesus and committing their lives to Him. See "How can I have hope?" (p. 53) for more about having a relationship with the Lord.

HOW DO I EXPERIENCE PEACE?

"You will keep in perfect peace all who trust in you, all
whose thoughts are fixed on you!" (Isaiah 26:3 NLT)

The key: Structured reflection upon God's Word

If you want to experience more peace and draw closer to God in your
grief, try meditating (reflecting) on God and making it a regular part of
your life.

This might help you

It is a practice that God's people have used for centuries to grow closer
to Him. And when they do, they also receive the comfort and security
that a close relationship with Him brings. Here's how you do it:

- Think about what God has done, either in the past for His people[12]
  or in your own life.

  "I cried out to God for help; I cried out to God to hear me.... Then
  I thought ... 'I will remember the deeds of the LORD; yes, I will
  remember your miracles of long ago. I will consider all your works
  and meditate on all your mighty deeds.'" (Psalm 77:1, 10–12)

- Reflect on a passage of Scripture. Think about how those words
  should affect the way you live your life. How can the teaching in the
  passage change *and* bless you? We encourage you to make a plan
  to read the Bible on a regular basis. You might start with Proverbs
  10–31 or the book of James. (If you do not have a Bible, you can use
  www.biblegateway.com.)

  "Blessed is the one who does not walk in step with the wicked or
  stand in the way that sinners take or sit in the company of mockers,
  but whose delight is in the law of the LORD, and who meditates on
  his law day and night. That person is like a tree planted by streams
  of water, which yields its fruit in season and whose leaf does not
  wither." (Psalm 1:1–3a)

- Record your thoughts about the Bible passage in a journal. If
  you're not sure what to write, here are some questions you can
  use as a guide:

---

12 God's people are those who have received His forgiveness and have committed to
   following His Word (the Bible) as they live their lives. See "How can I have hope?" (p. 53)
   for more about such a relationship with God.

GRIEF SHARE LOSS OF A SPOUSE

- What is the main point in the passage?
- If I applied its teaching in my life, how would it affect the way I usually think about life?
- If I used this teaching in my life, how would my behaviors or speech change?
- When was the last time I could have used this teaching? (If you did use it, jot down what happened. If you did not, jot down what you could have changed.)
- If I have difficulty applying this teaching, who might be able to help me with it?

A word of caution: Don't expect instant results from meditating on Bible passages. It may take time before you begin to experience peace and comfort from reflecting on God's Word. But if you do it consistently, you will gradually begin to notice a difference in the way you think about your circumstances. And that will lead you to enjoy increasing levels of hope and peace.

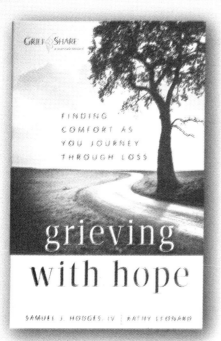

APPENDIX

CONTENTS

HOW CAN I HAVE HOPE?

"Brothers and sisters, we do not want you to be uninformed about those who sleep in death, so that you do not grieve like the rest of mankind, who have no hope." (1 Thessalonians 4:13)

God affirms your grief

When life is shattered by the death of a loved one, it's easy to descend into hopelessness. Your future plans revolved around having your spouse beside you, enjoying the triumphs and shouldering the tragedies *together*. But now what?

When the Apostle Paul wrote the verse above, he was writing to people who were grieving the death of loved ones. They were devastated. Their expectations for the future were shattered. They also wondered, Now what?

God, who inspired Paul's response, affirmed the people's grief. And God understands how *your* life has been turned upside down by the death of your spouse.

Yet, surprisingly, Paul also writes about grieving with hope (grieving the loss, but nevertheless confident there's something to look forward to in the future).

Hope might seem impossible

Grieving with hope might sound unreasonable. Your life can't continue the way you had planned. Any further planning might even seem pointless. There's so much uncertainty on many different levels, for example:

- Relationally: It may be hard to imagine ever having such a close relationship with someone else. Will there ever be someone with whom to dream again? Who you're confident "has your back"? Whom you can trust enough to discuss major decisions in your life?

- Physically: There is a renewed—and raw—sense of how fragile life is. An infection, tumor, or accident can change the course of your life without warning.

- Financially: Your household income may be cut significantly. How will household bills be paid on time?

Reflecting on these realities can generate worry upon worry about the upcoming weeks and months. If that's what you've experienced, you are not alone! Whenever we're faced with our limitations, the "what if" and "what now" questions start to churn in our minds.

But, as you think even further into the future, there might be another type of uncertainty that creeps into your mind. This uncertainty has to do with what will happen when you die.

How spiritual uncertainty contributes to hopelessness

What happens after death? What will it be like for you to face God? Some people "hope" they've been good enough to receive God's acceptance, but there remains a gnawing uncertainty. Others try to ignore the issue. But the prospect of facing God's judgment cannot be easily shaken. Indeed, it *shouldn't*, because the Bible reminds us that "people are destined to die once, and after that to face judgment" (Hebrews 9:27).

All of these types of uncertainty make it hard to understand how Paul could think that anyone can *grieve with hope*. How is it possible?

Before we go on, we understand that you might not be ready to think about what will happen when you die. It can be an uncomfortable topic to consider. So, if you aren't ready to contemplate this, set this article aside to finish later. But if you are open to giving this more thought, we encourage you to do so. This issue is vitally important. In fact, true and lasting hope is possible only if you wisely address this particular spiritual uncertainty.

Hope is possible if we go to God

The reason we must face judgment when we die is because all of us are morally imperfect and accountable to God for those imperfections. The Bible refers to our moral imperfections as *sins*. The word *sin* has been used in ways that are confusing and unnecessarily judgmental. But, simply put, sin is falling short of God's standards for us. And when we understand it that way, it helps us to see that while most of us like to think of ourselves as good people, in light of God's standards we all fall short. That's why the Bible says, "There is no one on earth who is righteous, no one who does what is right and never sins" (Ecclesiastes 7:20).

Now here's the problem: our sins aren't merely oversights or innocent mistakes on our part. Sin is supremely offensive to God! And this is why we deserve God's judgment.

The reason for hope

In His incredible mercy, God has made a way for us to be saved from the punishment that our sins deserve. That's why God sent Jesus to the earth. Jesus was the only man who ever lived who faced temptations but never sinned (Hebrews 4:15). When He was executed on the cross (on false charges), He offered Himself to God in our place. "For Christ also suffered once for sins, the righteous for the unrighteous, to bring you to God" (1 Peter 3:18). He received the punishment for our sins. And because of His sacrifice, it's possible for us to receive God's forgiveness (His pardon) for our sins!

Jesus' death was followed by His resurrection. With Jesus' resurrection from the dead, we get a preview of God's plan to fix *everything* that is wrong with the world. Eventually there will be no more sin to separate God's people from Him. There will be no more illnesses to wear down their bodies. There will be no more deaths to rip relationships apart. There will come a time for God's people when *all* the reasons for hopelessness will disappear! The Bible promises that someday Jesus "will wipe away every tear from their eyes, and death shall be no more, neither shall there be mourning, nor crying, nor pain anymore, for the former things have passed away" (Revelation 21:4 ESV).

How to receive God's forgiveness

God has provided you with the gift of forgiveness. How do you receive it? *By asking for His forgiveness of your sins, because of Jesus' death on the cross.* Here is a prayer you can use:

> Dear Lord, I confess that I'm not perfect. I know I deserve judgment. And I am so grateful that Jesus died for my sins. Please forgive me. Please help me now to live my life for Your purposes, not my own. In Jesus' name, amen.

That act of faith—completely depending upon Christ's death and resurrection to spare you from judgment—makes you part of God's family; He becomes your Heavenly Father. "See what kind of love the Father has given to us, that we should be called children of God; and so we are" (1 John 3:1 ESV). And as God's child, you have His promise that if you prioritize His purposes in your life, He will meet all of your needs.

> So do not worry, saying, "What shall we eat?" or "What shall we drink?" or "What shall we wear?" For the pagans run after all these things, and your heavenly Father knows that you need them. But

seek first his kingdom and his righteousness, and all these things will be given to you as well. (Matthew 6:31–33)

Being adopted into God's family is now the start of a brand-new adventure in your life. In order to learn more about this adventure, you need to get involved in a local Bible-teaching church. Talk to your Loss of a Spouse host or to the pastor of the church that sponsored Loss of a Spouse. They can help you find a church to help you grow in your relationship with the Lord.

FREE DAILY EMAIL ENCOURAGEMENT

as you rebuild your life

SIGN UP AND RECEIVE AN UPLIFTING EMAIL MESSAGE EACH DAY FOR A YEAR.

"I can't begin to tell you how helpful these messages are— perfect timing, straight to the heart."

"The daily emails from GriefShare are one of the first things I look for each morning."

Learn more at www.griefshare.org.

IS MY GRIEF NORMAL?

Grief is a naturally unpleasant experience that affects your body, your thinking, and your emotions. Unfortunately, living in a world where losses occur, grief is also unavoidable. But you might be surprised by how grief is affecting you. Look at the following chart, which describes both common grief reactions and potential problems. If you are concerned about how you're reacting to the loss of your spouse, talk to your pastor, a physician, or a Christian counselor.

Grief Reaction	What's Normal	What Could Be a Problem
Sadness and loneliness	Crying, sometimes unexpectedly A profound sense of loss & what you'll miss in your life Yearning (strong desire) for your spouse	There are no breaks in the feelings of sadness (no memories of funny events that can break the tension of sadness) Avoiding people for days Apathy ("I don't care about anything")
Anger	Upset over your spouse's choice not to get help (soon enough) Dissatisfaction with your spouse's professional care Regret over your response to your spouse's death Regret over choices you made for your spouse Upset over being left alone Dissatisfaction with God letting this happen	You entertain thoughts of harming yourself You entertain thoughts of harming others You are so irritable with people that they are no longer stopping by You are often agitated because you keep thinking about how unfair your loss is You refuse to pray, go to church, read your Bible **Continued ...**

Grief Reaction	What's Normal	What Could Be a Problem
Anxiety or worry	Feeling jittery or "on edge" most of the time Thinking about what might happen with a sense of dread Being unsure that you can do everything that needs to be done (feeling helpless) Being more aware of your own vulnerability	Panic attacks Unable to turn off "what if" thinking Avoiding people for days Not leaving your house or apartment for days
Shock	An initial sense that the death is not real A numbness (not having any feelings you can identify)	An unwillingness to accept the death or the changes that need to be made
Relief	Especially after a spouse's chronic illness, feeling relaxed, because the burden of care is lifted A sense of freedom from a grueling schedule of caregiving After a difficult marriage, a sense of being released from unrealistic expectations	Feeling guilty or ashamed because of feeling relaxed or free
Guilt	Thoughts like "I didn't do enough for my spouse." Thoughts like "I wish I'd said/done ____." Thoughts like "I wish I hadn't said/done ___."	Not being able to resolve negative thinking about yourself **Continued ...**

GRIEF SHARE LOSS OF A SPOUSE

Grief Reaction	What's Normal	What Could Be a Problem
Problems with memory and concentration	Difficulty focusing your attention on tasks Difficulty making decisions Difficulty remembering what people say or what you wanted to do	Bills might not get paid Hasty decisions might be made Appointments might be missed
Physical concerns	Stomach pain Headache Neck pain Chest pain/racing heartbeat Tightening in the throat Muscle weakness	Only a physician can diagnose a medical problem. If you experience these symptoms, make an appointment with your doctor. Tell your physician about the symptoms and about your loss.

RECEIVING GOD'S FORGIVENESS

Bitterness against your spouse can prolong your grief. So, forgiving your spouse of any offenses is part of dealing with your grief. But what about your contributions to unresolved conflict in your relationship? How do you receive forgiveness?

Ultimately, you are accountable to God: "'As surely as I live,' says the Lord, 'every knee will bow before me; every tongue will acknowledge God.' So then, each of us will give an account of ourselves to God" (Romans 14:11–12). God has provided for your forgiveness through Jesus.

Jesus' death on the cross paid the debt of sin you could not pay. If you trust in Christ's sufficient payment for your sin, then ask God to forgive you based on what Christ did for you. That act of faith makes you part of God's family; He becomes your Heavenly Father. "See what kind of love the Father has given to us, that we should be called children of God; and so we are" (1 John 3:1a ESV).

So, then, God's children are a *forgiven* people. And for that reason, their Heavenly Father expects them to be *forgiving* people when others offend them. This is why Jesus makes the startling comment in Matthew 6:15: "But if you do not forgive others their sins, your Father will not forgive your sins." To withhold forgiveness after having received God's gracious forgiveness contradicts God's gift.

Jesus' perspective on forgiveness is a testimony to how great God's gift of forgiveness is. To receive His forgiveness is life-changing; it fosters the same kind of gracious attitude God shows to us.[13]

13 For more information on God's gift of forgiveness, see "How can I have hope?" (p. 53).

FINANCIAL AND LEGAL ACTION STEPS AFTER THE DEATH OF A SPOUSE

1. Contact the funeral home to make arrangements. In addition, ask about getting copies of the death certificate. You may need as many as a dozen, depending on the agencies that might require to have one on file. (Ask if the agencies *need* a certified copy on record or if seeing a photocopy would be acceptable, because certified copies might be expensive.)

2. Collect birth certificate, marriage license or certificate, and insurance policies to have on hand for changing or closing accounts, transferring assets, etc.

3. Contact your spouse's employer. Speak with the company's human resources department for getting any needed paperwork. (Make sure you have your spouse's Social Security card or number.)

4. Contact an attorney about reviewing the will (or to learn about the probate process).

5. Organize a list of the regular household bills that will need to be paid. Have the bills put in your name.

6. If you don't have experience managing finances, you would be wise to enlist the help of a financial planner. You should do so cautiously, however. There are many people who call themselves "financial planners," but who actually have products and investments they'd like to sell you. You should look for a "fee-based Certified Financial Planner (CFP)." This is someone who is legally required to offer advice that is in your best interest. This person will help you develop a budget and plan for the future.

7. Contact the bank and credit card companies to have all joint accounts put in your name.

8. Contact all insurance companies to have all joint accounts put in your name. Contact life insurance providers, if applicable, to complete their paperwork (benefits can take several weeks to start). Contact the health insurance company if your spouse was under medical care just prior to death to file a claim for expenses.

9. Contact the Social Security Administration to see if you are eligible for any benefits. Ask about getting a copy of your spouse's last benefits statement. In the US, your Social Security options can be complex, so you may also wish to speak with a financial planner or attorney experienced in Social Security benefits. If you live in Canada, you'll be dealing with the Canada Pension Plan, but the advice for getting help is similar.

10. Contact the Department of Veterans Affairs, if applicable, regarding any benefits. Ask about getting a copy of your spouse's last benefits statement.

11. Update deeds and titles to have only your name listed: home, automobiles, etc.

GRIEF&SHARE® RESOURCES

GriefShare support groups

Attend a weekly GriefShare support group, where you can share your emotions in a safe place and learn helpful insights on how to walk the journey of grief. To find a list of groups near you, go to **GriefShare.org**.

A Season of Grief free daily email messages

Receive an encouraging email message every day for a year. Sign up for these free messages at **GriefShare.org/dailyemails**. You can also email a friend who is hurting and encourage him or her to sign up. (The messages are an online version of the book *Through a Season of Grief*.)

Through a Season of Grief devotional

This book of 365 short, daily messages is based on the GriefShare program. Each day you will be equipped with biblical comfort and practical teaching to help you take steps forward toward healing. Look for *Through a Season of Grief* by Bill Dunn and Kathy Leonard at a local or online bookstore or at **GriefShare.org/devotional**.

Grieving with Hope

This powerful, GriefShare-based book contains short, topical chapters addressing issues that grieving people face but are often hesitant to mention to others; it helps people accurately interpret the message their emotions are sending them and gently guides them to determine whether they're grieving in a way that leads to hope and ultimate healing. Look for *Grieving with Hope* by Samuel Hodges and Kathy Leonard at a local or online bookstore or at **GriefShare.org/hope**.

Tell a friend about GriefShare

If you know someone hurting because of loss, make sure he or she knows about GriefShare by using the share tools at **GriefShare.org**. You can share a GriefShare page via email or your social networks.

How to help grieving children

If you have school-age children dealing with grief, the "How to Help Grieving Children" video offers suggestions and helps answer tough questions you might have in caring for them. View this video at **GriefShare.org/children**.

Surviving the Holidays seminars

Surviving the Holidays seminars are offered during the Thanksgiving and Christmas season. This seminar helps you reduce stress, minimize loneliness, and discover a healthy approach to the holiday season after your spouse's death. At **GriefShare.org/holidays** you can search for a group meeting near you. You'll also find articles, real-life stories, and video clips to help you through the stresses of facing the holidays without your spouse.

Other online help

At **GriefShare.org**, print and use the "Help for the Journey" personal Bible study, read the "God, What Is Going On?" pages, and learn more about the GriefShare program. Find helpful videos at the GriefShare YouTube channel, **YouTube.com/griefshare**. Visit our Facebook page at **Facebook.com/griefshare**.